W9-BHB-988

Celebrity Entrepreneurs

JENNIFER LOPEZ

Kate Shoup

Cavendish
Square

New York

For Heidi
Published in 2015 by Cavendish Square Publishing, LLC
243 5th Avenue, Suite 136, New York, NY 10016

Website: cavendishsq.com

This publication represents the opinions and views of the author based on his or her personal experience, knowledg and research. The information in this book serves as a general guide only. The author and publisher have used the best efforts in preparing this book and disclaim liability rising directly or indirectly from the use and applicatior of this book.

CPSIA Compliance Information: Batch #WW15CSQ

All websites were available and accurate when this book was sent to press.

Library of Congress Cataloging-in-Publication Data

Shoup, Kate, 1972-
Jennifer Lopez / Kate Shoup.
pages cm. — (Celebrity entrepreneurs)
Includes index.
ISBN 978-1-50260-004-2 (hardcover) ISBN 978-1-50260-026-4 (paperback) ISBN 978-1-50260-033-2 (eboc
1. Lopez, Jennifer, 1970- 2. Motion picture actors and actresses—United States—Biography. 3. Singers—
United States—Biography. I. Title.
PN2287.L634S57 2015
791.4302'8092—dc23
[B]
2014031012

Editor: Kristen Susienka
Copy Editor: Cynthia Roby
Art Director: Jeffrey Talbot
Designer: Joseph Macri
Senior Production Manager: Jennifer Ryder-Talbot
Production Editor: David McNamara
Photo Researcher: J8 Media

Printed in the United States of America

CONTENTS

Jennifer Lopez is one of the most successful celebrity entrepreneurs today.

J. Lo's American Dream

Perhaps more than any other performer today, Jennifer Lopez signifies the American Dream. Raised in a working-class Bronx neighborhood, Jennifer Lopez, or J. Lo, as her fans call her, has risen to become one of the biggest stars in the world. Today she is known not only for her singing talent but also for the many areas of business in which she is involved, from beauty and designer clothing lines to perfumes, acting, and mobile phones. Her story is proof that if you have enough ambition and determination, you too can become a part of the business world.

Although her parents discouraged her from pursuing a career as an entertainer, Jennifer was determined to succeed. Jennifer, as of 2014, has acted in more than thirty movies, earning more than $1.4 billion at the box office. On top of that, she has released eight record albums with sales totaling more than $55 million. Incredibly, in 2001, she became the first, and only, person to have a number one album and film, *J. Lo* and *The Wedding Planner*, respectively, in the same week!

Jennifer Lopez is so much more than a performer, however. She is also the head of a multi-million dollar business empire. With a hand in home décor, fashion, fragrance, film production, mobile phones, and more, Jennifer has shown that she is not just a singer, dancer, and actress. She's also a global **brand** and an inspiration to many.

Jennifer's impact on the world has been tremendous, particularly among the Latino and Hispanic communities. She is regarded as one of the most influential performers in the United States, hence *People en Español* naming her "Most Influential Hispanic" in 2007. Jennifer's success has helped to empower the Latin American community, and has inspired countless entertainers of Latin descent, including actress Jessica Alba and singer Kat DeLuna. However, it's not just Hispanics or Latinos who look to Jennifer as an example.

Her success as both a performer and an **entrepreneur** has blazed a trail for young stars such as Taylor Swift, Katy Perry, and more. Jennifer also "gives back" through her charitable organization, The Lopez Family Foundation, which is, in its own words, "dedicated to improving the health and well-being of women and children."

Of course, it hasn't always been smooth sailing for Jennifer. There have been plenty of bumps in the road on the artistic side, in business, and in her personal life. In the mid 2000s, her popularity as a musician and an actress plummeted, her albums underperformed on the charts, and her movies failed at the box office. Critics described *Gigli* (2003), in which she starred alongside then-fiancé Ben Affleck, as "the worst movie of all time." Similar failures plagued Jennifer's business ventures, most notably, two of her clothing lines. She was forced to shut down production in 2008 and 2009. Her challenging personal life, which attracted widespread media attention, offered little rest. Three marriages and various other high-profile relationships were no doubt a drain.

Jennifer didn't let these unexpected events keep her down, however. "I can take a lot of punches and still keep going," she has said. "I've been trained like a boxer to go fifteen rounds." This attitude enabled Jennifer to mount an extraordinary comeback. In 2010, she partnered with Tommy Hilfiger to design the Jennifer Lopez Collection and the Jennifer Lopez Home Collection. That same year, she joined *American Idol* as a panelist. Thanks to the exposure she received on the show, Jennifer was soon asked to be an ambassador for several popular brands, including L'Oreal, Gillette, Fiat, and TOUS Jewelry. Likewise, her fragrance collection continued to grow, with more than $2 billion in total sales. Within just two years, in 2012, Jennifer found herself in the No. 1 slot on the *Forbes* Celebrity 100, which tracks the world's most powerful celebrities. Jennifer, who currently has more than 28.4 million Twitter followers and more than 42,000,000 "likes" on Facebook, was back!

How has Jennifer Lopez managed to become a successful musician, actress, and entrepreneur? The answer is simple: her incredible work ethic. A self-described workaholic, she has said that, "You get what you give. What you put into things is what you get out of them." She has credited her parents

Jennifer Lopez is back ... and she's better than ever!

for setting a great example: "With my mom and dad, I really did get the feeling we could do anything if we worked hard enough."

Despite her fame and her incredible success, Jennifer has never forgotten her roots. Where she came from is as much a part of her identity as where she's gone. Even with dozens of films, eight record albums, countless awards and nominations, and several entrepreneurial endeavors, Jennifer always remembers home, the place where it all started.

Young Jennifer Lopez
in high school.

Chapter One

From the Bronx to the Big Time

Long before she began her career as a film actress and musician, before she launched a fashion and fragrance empire, or unveiled her own production company, was named a judge on *American Idol*, or became the highest-paid Latina actress in history, Jennifer Lynn Lopez was, in her own words, "Jenny from the block."

Bronx Beginnings

By "block," Jennifer meant her neighborhood, Castle Hill, located in the south-central section of the Bronx, a **borough** of New York City. It was there that the Lopez family lived, first in a small apartment and later in a modest two-story home on Blackrock Avenue, where

Jennifer shared a room with her two sisters, Lynda and Leslie. To support the family, her father, David, worked the night shift at Guardian Insurance Company, and later became a computer technician. Her mother, Guadalupe, sold Tupperware and worked as a kindergarten teacher at Jennifer's school. Like many residents of Castle Hill, David and Guadalupe had emigrated from Puerto Rico.

Jennifer attended Catholic school and excelled in athletics. She participated in gymnastics, track, and softball. However, her real passions were singing and dancing. She took lessons in both early on. Jennifer also enjoyed acting. During her senior year at Preston High School, she auditioned for a low-budget film, *My Little Girl*, and was thrilled to be cast in the role of Myra.

While her parents were no doubt proud of Jennifer's accomplishment, they discouraged her from a career in the arts. To them, Jennifer's dream of becoming a star was not a practical career path. To please them, Jennifer enrolled at Manhattan's Baruch College in 1987, where she studied law. It was a doomed effort, however. "I didn't want to go to college—I wanted to try to dance full time," she later told

W Magazine. She dropped out after only one semester, determined to pursue her dream.

Jennifer's Early Career

Early in her career as a performer, Jennifer won roles in a few regional stage productions. She then performed in the chorus of a show called *Golden Musicals of Broadway*, during which she spent five months on tour in Europe. After that came a stint as a dancer, singer, and **choreographer** in Japan. In 1991, the famous boy band New Kids on the Block selected Jennifer as a backup dancer. Later, she would also work as a backup dancer for Janet Jackson.

Her big break came in 1991, when she beat out 2,000 other applicants for a spot on the popular television show *In Living Color* as a dancer, or "Fly Girl." A popular sketch-comedy show, *In Living Color* featured many African American and other diverse performers. In addition to Jennifer, several other famous entertainers got their start on the show, including Jamie Foxx and Jim Carrey. Thrilled, Jennifer moved to Los Angeles to begin filming. Working under choreographer Rosie Perez, a famous Latina performer, she enjoyed two seasons on the show.

Jennifer Lopez (right) on the set of *In Living Color.*

The Transition to Acting

Although Jennifer enjoyed her time as a
Fly Girl, she quit *In Living Color* in 1993
to pursue acting. Her early efforts met with
failure, however. In 1993, CBS cast her in
the television series *Second Chances*, but it
was cancelled after only ten episodes. Her
appearance on a second show, *Hotel Malibu*,
encountered a similar fate. Jennifer no doubt
became discouraged, but she persevered.

In 1995, Jennifer landed a role in the film
My Family, and her performance earned her a
nomination for an Independent Spirit Award.
That same year, she starred alongside Wesley
Snipes and Woody Harrelson in *Money Train*.

Selena

The movie *Selena* was a **biopic** about a famous Latina singer, Selena Quintanilla, who came from Texas. After releasing her first album at the age of twelve, Selena recorded fourteen top-ten singles in the Top Latin Songs chart,

The Queen of *Tejano* music, Selena Quintanilla. Jennifer portrayed Selena in a biopic about the slain star.

including seven number-one hits. Called the "Queen of *Tejano* music," Selena sold 60 million albums worldwide, and is the third best-selling Latin American artist of all time.

Sadly, Selena was shot and killed on March 31, 1995. She was twenty-three years old. Shockingly, Selena's killer, Yolanda Saldívar, had been the president of Selena's fan club. The murder occurred when Selena confronted Saldívar after discovering that she had stolen funds from the club. Some 60,000 mourners attended Selena's funeral. For her part, Saldívar was sentenced to life in prison.

In 1996, famed director Francis Ford Coppola cast her in the movie *Jack* with Robin Williams and Diane Lane, among others.

More films would follow, over thirty in all. Some, such as *Selena*, *Out of Sight*, and *The Wedding Planner*, were great successes. Others, however, struggled. The movie *Gigli*, for example, received harsh reviews and was considered a flop.

Becoming a Musician

Inspired during the filming of *Selena*, Jennifer decided to record a **demo**. It was sent to Sony Music, who quickly signed Jennifer to its Work Group label. In 1999, she began work on her first album, *On the 6*. Aware that many believed she had merely taken advantage of her fame and beauty to secure her record deal, she was desperate to demonstrate her musical talent. The album's first single, "If You Had My Love," provided the necessary proof. It shot to the top of the *Billboard* Hot 100.

Jennifer would go on to release several more albums. For inspiration, she drew from musical genres including Latin, pop, dance, R&B, hip-hop, rock, funk, house, and salsa. To date, her total album sales top $55 million. She has also won three American Music Awards, several

Billboard Music Awards and *Billboard* Latin Music Awards, and has been nominated for two Grammy Awards.

Jennifer did more than release several hit albums of her own. Starting in 2010, she helped aspiring performers land their own record deals as a judge on the popular television show *American Idol.* In 2014, she signed on for her fourth season with the show, for an estimated $17.5 million. One thing was clear, Jenny was a long way from the block!

The cover for Jennifer's first album, *On the 6.*

Jennifer, in 2014, hosting a runway show featuring her designs.

Chapter Two

Becoming an Entrepreneur

For Jennifer Lopez, being an iconic dancer, singer, and actress was not enough. She wanted to be an entrepreneur, too. To do this, she needed to break into more industries, ones that could reach wider audiences and embrace new trends—such as fashion and beauty.

"It's Time to Wear My Look"

In 1998, she launched a fashion line, J. Lo by Jennifer Lopez. Later, this line would be replaced with one called Just Sweet. Fashion was a natural fit for Jennifer, whose memorable outfits often made headlines. As Jennifer said during the launch of her fashions, "It's time for the world to wear my look!"

Designing clothes was a dream come true. "From the time I was little, I would get a whacked pair of pants, really cheap, cut them up and make a beautiful tiny miniskirt out of them," Jennifer said. Of particular interest was offering clothes for all women, large and small. Jennifer explained, "I find it is difficult for women who are curvaceous to find clothes in stores that fit. I want to offer clothes that are wonderfully designed and will fit women of all sizes."

Soon, Jennifer's fashion line expanded to include swimwear, eyewear, jewelry, footwear, accessories, handbags, and more. She also built a sportswear line for girls, which included tops, shorts, skirts, and jeans. A high-end clothing line, Sweetface, was launched in 2005 and rounded out her portfolio.

In 2010, she partnered with designer Tommy Hilfiger and Kohl's department store to launch the Jennifer Lopez Collection, a new line of clothing and accessories. The Jennifer Lopez Home Collection, featuring bedding, towels, and luggage, soon followed. Another partnership—this one with fashion designer Erica Zohar—created Teeology, Inc., a

Move Over, Barbie!

In 2013, American toy manufacturing company Mattel® released two Jennifer Lopez Barbie dolls. "Barbie has grown into all different ethnicities," Jennifer said of the Latina version of the doll. "I thought it was important to have a Latina Barbie, but a Latina Barbie that was real. I wanted to make sure that the hair ... the nose, the cheekbones, were real." The Red Carpet doll has a pouting mouth while the World Tour doll has a broad smile. Each was modeled to be a true-life expression of Jennifer onstage. The outfits the dolls wear are authentic miniatures of dresses Jennifer Lopez has worn. "It hasn't really sunk in yet—that I am a part of the Barbie family," Jennifer, who was thinking of her own daughter, Emme, when helping to design the dolls, said. "I wanted her to play with a doll made in her likeness."

Los Angeles-based electronic commerce company that sells luxury T-shirts for men and women designed by various artists.

How Sweet It Smells: Jennifer's Fragrance Empire

In 2002, Jennifer was ready to expand her brand. In collaboration with perfume company Coty Inc., she released her own fragrance, Glow by J. Lo. She described the perfume as "a true reflection of the modern, independent, yet passionate woman." The scent was described as "clean" and "soapy," with **notes** of orange, pink grapefruit, rose, sandalwood, amber, musk, jasmine, iris, and vanilla. Soon, Jennifer and Coty collaborated to create yet more fragrances—to date, there are eighteen different scents. Her most recent perfume, Glowing, is described as an "evolution" of the original Glow.

From Actress to Producer

After acting for some time, Jennifer wanted to experience show business through a different lens: that of a producer. She formed her own film and television production company,

Jennifer at the launch for her perfume Glowing in 2012.

Nuyorican Productions, in 2001. The word "Nuyorican" is a **portmanteau** of the words "New York" and "Puerto Rican." Although the term was initially used as an insult, leading artists of Puerto Rican descent claimed it as their own, thereby transforming its meaning. In time, poets, writers, musicians, and visual artists proudly identified themselves as Nuyorican. Jennifer chose "Nuyorican" as the name of her production company to honor her own background as a New Yorker of Puerto Rican descent.

Jennifer outside the flagship VivaMóvil store in Brooklyn, New York in 2013.

In 2003, Nuyorican Productions partnered with HBO on the documentary *Los Quinces*, about a ball traditionally held to commemorate a Cuban girl's fifteenth birthday. Three years later, the company produced the primetime television drama *South Beach* for the UPN network. Other projects, including films (*Bordertown*, *El Cantante*, and *Dance Again*), a mini-series broadcast on Univision, and a show that aired on Fox, soon followed. More recent ventures include *The Fosters* on ABC and *South Beach Tow* on truTV.

Due in part to her experience as a producer, nuvoTV, a cable television channel that caters to the Latino community, approached Jennifer in 2013 to serve as its chief creative officer. In that role, she manages marketing and program production, and occasionally appears on the air.

VivaMóvil

In 2013 Jennifer Lopez co-founded VivaMóvil, a mobile phone retailer. The goal of the venture is to provide a better retail experience for the growing Latino market, which was estimated to have had $1.2 trillion in purchasing power in 2012. The company's flagship store, in Brooklyn, New York, boasts a vibrant décor, and a play area for children, all designed with Latin appeal. Additional stores in Los Angeles and Miami are planned.

Jennifer accepts
the Icon Award at
the 2014 *Billboard*
Music Awards.

Chapter Three

Through Good Times and Bad

In the nearly twenty-five years since Jennifer Lopez debuted as a Fly Girl on *In Living Color*, she has become more than just a dancer, singer, actress, and entrepreneur. She has become a cultural **icon**. Indeed, in May 2014, Jennifer won the Icon Award at the *Billboard* Music Awards, the first woman and Latina to do so. "You continue to break down barriers and inspire girls," pop star Rihanna told Jennifer in a video montage shown during the award show broadcast.

In her acceptance speech, Jennifer delivered a special message to her young fans: "All you little ones sitting on the living room floor watching the TV right now, just like I used to do when I was back in the Bronx, have faith, dream big, think big, and know that anything is possible!"

Business Successes

While the *Billboard* Icon Award commemorated Jennifer's achievements as a musician, dancer, and actress, including her tremendous popularity in recent years as a judge on *American Idol*, those aren't the only areas in which she has excelled. She has also had tremendous success as a businesswoman.

Perhaps her most successful business venture has been her line of fragrances. Although many predicted that her first scent, Glow by J. Lo (2003), would fail, it generated more than $100 million in sales in its first year alone, becoming the top-selling fragrance in America. The success of Glow inspired Jennifer to further create seventeen additional fragrances for her line. While some of the scents are completely new, others are **flankers**—that is, perfumes that are subtle variations of an existing perfume. In total, sales of Jennifer's fragrance line have exceeded $2 billion.

Bernd Beetz, CEO of Coty, notes, "Our launch of Glow … was a defining moment for both our company and the industry, reinventing the celebrity fragrance category." Other celebrities quickly took note of Jennifer's success as a **parfumier**. Before long, stars such as Taylor Swift, Beyoncé, Lady Gaga, and many more would follow in her footsteps, releasing their own perfumes.

Jennifer has also served as an ambassador of several popular brands, including L'Oreal, Gillette, Fiat, and TOUS Jewelry. As noted by Jon Albert, a leading celebrity talent broker, "[Jennifer's] beautiful, talented, multicultural, a movie actress, and an entrepreneur. A lot of people like her. That makes her an excellent spokesperson, particularly to female consumers."

Bumps in the Road

No doubt, Jennifer has enjoyed tremendous success. As you've read, she's sold more than 80 million records worldwide, earned more than $1.4 billion at the box office, and oversees a fashion and fragrance empire. However, it hasn't all been smooth sailing.

In 2002, Jennifer suffered from exhaustion. "I was very overworked and I was doing music and movies and so many things," she explained.

"I was suffering from a lack of sleep." After time to rest and reflect, Jennifer was soon back to business.

In addition, some of Jennifer's business involvements—artistic and entrepreneurial—had failed. On the artistic side, a few of her albums, including *Como Ama una Mujer* (2007) and *Brave* (2007), underperformed on the charts. Likewise, several movies in a row failed to meet expectations. Several critics, as you read, viewed *Gigli* (2003) as "the worst movie of all time." Film critic Richard Roeper described the film as "a disaster … one of the worst movies I've ever seen."

Jennifer, however, took these failures in stride. "I don't know anyone who bats a thousand in the movie business," she said. "I've made some great movies, and I've made some not-so-great movies."

Her production company, Nuyorican Productions, suffered similar setbacks. The show *South Beach* (2006) experienced low ratings and received generally negative reviews. In addition, the film *Bordertown* (2006) made just $8 million—$13 million less than it cost to produce.

Jennifer Lopez at the 2003 premiere of her movie *Gigli*. The movie was not a success.

On the business side, two of Jennifer's clothing lines, Just Sweet and Sweetface, shut down in 2008 and 2009, respectively. Jennifer was discouraged, and later admitted that she simply didn't understand the fashion business well enough when she started the lines. It's worth noting, however, that the Jennifer Lopez Collection and the Jennifer Lopez Home Collection at Kohl's are thriving. Jennifer often wears pieces from the clothing line in the *American Idol* studio.

Personal Life

Jennifer's personal life has attracted widespread media attention. Of particular interest is her multiple marriages and romantic relationships. Her first marriage, to Cuban waiter Ojani Noa, ended in 1998, after just eleven months. In 1999, Jennifer began dating Sean Combs. Like Jennifer, Sean was a performer and entrepreneur. The couple eventually split, however.

A second marriage, to backup dancer Cris Judd in 2001, lasted just over a year. After divorcing Judd, Jennifer became engaged to actor Ben Affleck, but the wedding, scheduled for September 2003, was cancelled. In June of 2004, Jennifer wed Latino recording artist and long-time friend Marc Anthony. It seemed the marriage would last—Jennifer and Marc appeared deeply in love and had two children, twins Max and Emme—but unfortunately, the couple separated in 2011.

After her split with Marc Anthony, Jennifer enjoyed a two-and-a-half year relationship with dancer and choreographer Casper Smart—although that relationship has since ended. "It's about finding a relationship that has enough good stuff to outweigh the bad," she told *Glamour UK*. "If something doesn't feel right to me or makes me feel uncomfortable, I don't want to go along with it—and sometimes as women we do that. But I won't accept it anymore."

"I'm Going to Get Back Up"

Even when things go wrong, Jennifer tries not to let it keep her down. "At this point," she said, "I can say to myself, 'So what if I fall? So what? I'm going to get back up.'" Film director Taylor Hackford, who directed Jennifer in the 2013 film *Parker*, says, "Whatever the odds are against her, she's never going to give up."

It's the "getting back up ... never giving up" attitude that defines Jennifer. It explains how, after setbacks in her personal and professional life, Jennifer was able to mount an extraordinary comeback. In 2012, Jennifer found herself at No. 1 on the *Forbes* Celebrity 100, which tracks the world's most powerful celebrities. If the past is any indication of her success, Jennifer's future is bright!

Jennifer Lopez isn't afraid of failure. If she gets knocked down, she gets back up!

Chapter Four

Looking to the Future

How has Jennifer Lopez become a successful musician, selling millions of records worldwide? How has she found fame as an actress, with some thirty films on her résumé? How has she launched a business empire, with interests in fashion, fragrance, and phones?

The Importance of Work Ethic

Jennifer has managed all of her successes through an unparalleled work ethic, lessons she learned from her parents. "My mom always told me that if you work hard, you can achieve anything," she said. "And it's true. It's one of the truest things ever." The *Los Angeles Times* points to Jennifer's strong personality, noting,

In February 2008, Jennifer gave birth to twins Maximilian and Emme. Of them, Jennifer has said, "They make everything better in my life," adding, "[Being a] mommy—it's just the one thing you don't want to mess up. You can mess up in all other areas and get back up, but you can't mess up there." Jennifer has coped by stepping back from projects that just aren't important to her. "I'm at a point in my life when I just don't feel the need to put out anything unless I totally, absolutely feel it says what I want to say," Jennifer said.

In 2013, Jennifer received the Grace Kelly Award at the eighth annual March of Dimes luncheon. She was recognized as a celebrity parent role model supporting women giving birth to healthy babies after full-term pregnancies.

"It's hard to think of a more emblematic figure of multitasking modern celebrity." For Jennifer, hard work has paid off!

Jennifer's Influence

Jennifer has made a tremendous impact on the world. Perhaps nowhere has this impact been more strongly felt than in the Hispanic and Latin communities. As the highest-paid actress of Latin American descent, Jennifer is generally regarded as the most influential Latina performer in America. It's an honor that Jennifer takes seriously.

"Being an example to others is a big part of my work," she has said. "We're realizing our power. We're realizing that we matter here," she has said, about the Latino community. "We're not just … the guys working behind the scenes in the kitchen and as a plumber."

Several entertainers of Latin American descent have cited Jennifer as an inspiration in their own work. Actress Jessica Alba notes that Jennifer "opened doors for ethnic girls like me," a sentiment shared by Kat DeLuna, who has said that Jennifer "paved the way for Latinas." Other performers, including Kerry Washington and Beyoncé, working women, moms—the list goes on—also find her empowering.

Jennifer has done more than just inspire others, however. According to *Vogue Magazine*, she has "changed the face of modern celebrity … what J. Lo really did was broaden the possibilities of what a superstar can be: a global brand." *Forbes* agrees: "She's everywhere—from cosmetics and automobiles, to catering and telecommunications. Over the past few years, J. Lo has grown into one of the most complex brands in the world."

What's Next for Jennifer?

If history is any guide, 2015 will see Jennifer working as hard as ever. Already, she has three films on her schedule: *The Boy Next Door*, *Home*, and *Lila and Eve*. A concert documentary is tentatively planned, and she's also signed to take on a role in *Shades of Blue*, a police drama produced by her *American Idol* **compatriot** Ryan Seacrest and set to air on NBC.

What about long term? Jennifer has said that she wants a long career, like those of such luminaries as Cher, Tina Turner, and other women who, as Jennifer noted, "came a

Jennifer with fellow actress Jessica Alba in 2008.

generation before this one and showed us that you don't have to, as a young woman, have an expiration date … you can do what you want into your sixties and seventies and you can be powerful and be vulnerable and be human."

Whatever is next for Jennifer, it will be on her terms. As she told *Billboard Magazine* during a 2014 interview, "I don't feel like I have anything to prove anymore." With dozens of films, an Independent Spirit Award, a Golden Globe nomination, eight albums, three American Music Awards, several *Billboard* Music Awards and *Billboard* Latin Music Awards, a *Billboard* Icon Award, and two Grammy nominations, not to mention a successful fashion and home line, a flourishing line of fragrances, and other entrepreneurial endeavors, "Jenny from the block" has more than proven her worth!

Making a Difference: The Lopez Family Foundation

A health scare for Jennifer's daughter, Emme, inspired Jennifer to create a charitable foundation. "She had this lump on her head," she told CNN. "It was kind

of soft and felt like water a little bit." Fortunately, Emme was fine, but Jennifer realized that many other children were not so lucky—particularly those who lacked access to proper and affordable medical care. "What if I didn't have access to great health care?" she said. "What if I was a mom just sitting there and there was something wrong with my baby and there was nothing I could do about it?" The Lopez Family Foundation was born.

The foundation's goal is to "dramatically increase the availability of quality health care and health education for women and children, regardless of their ability to pay," according to its website. One way it achieves its aims is through **telemedicine**. "I have lots of big dreams and envision big changes toward proper health care, prenatal care, pediatric care," said Jennifer.

Career Highlights Timeline

1969 Born in the Bronx, New York

1974 Begins singing and dancing lessons

1986 Cast as Myra in *My Little Girl*

1991 Cast as a Fly Girl dancer

1997 The film *Selena* is released

1999 *On the 6,* Jennifer's first album, is released

2001 Jennifer's second album, *J. Lo,* is released

2001 Launches J. Lo by Jennifer Lopez, her first fashion line; *The Wedding Planner* is released; Nuyorican Productions is launched

2002 Third album, *This Is Me…Now*, is released

2003 Launches her first perfume, Glow by J. Lo

2009 Forms The Lopez Family Foundation

2010 Launches the Jennifer Lopez Collection

2011 Joins Season 10 of the hit TV show *American Idol*

2014 Wins a *Billboard* Icon Award— the first woman and Latina to do so; performs at 2014 World Cup opening ceremonies with recording artist Pitbull

Glossary

biopic A biographical movie.

borough A subdivision of a city. New York City is divided into five boroughs: Manhattan, Staten Island, Brooklyn, Queens, and the Bronx.

brand A name, term, design, symbol, or any other feature that identifies one seller's product distinct from those of other sellers.

choreographer A person who plans and arranges dance movements.

compatriot Though this typically refers to a person from the same country as someone else, it can also mean simply a friend or a colleague.

demo A recording that demonstrates the capabilities of a musician or musical group.

entrepreneur Someone who starts and runs his or her own business.

flanker A new perfume that is a subtle variation of an existing perfume.

icon A person who is extremely successful and widely admired.

note In the context of perfume or fragrance, the origin of the aromas that can be perceived.

parfumier A person who creates or sells perfume.

portmanteau A combination of two or more words to create a new word.

***Tejano* music** Also called Tex-Mex music. The name given to a style of music popular among Mexican-American inhabitants of central and southern Texas.

telemedicine The use of telecommunications technology to diagnose and treat patients from a remote location.

Further Information

Books

Asselin, Kristine Carlson. *Jennifer Lopez: Actress & Pop Superstar*. Minneapolis, MN: ABDO Publishing, 2013.

Lopez, Jennifer. *True Love*. New York, NY: Celebra, 2014.

Tracy, Kathleen. *Jennifer Lopez: A Biography*. Westport, CT: Greenwood Press, 2008.

Woog, Adam. *Jennifer Lopez*. New York, NY: Chelsea House, 2008.

Websites

American Idol
www.americanidol.com
For the latest on *American Idol*, including videos of Jennifer in action, visit the show's official website.

J. Lo

www.jenniferlopez.com
For news, photos of Jennifer, and her latest videos, visit this, her official website.

The Lopez Family Foundation

lopezfamilyfoundation.org
Visit this site to find out how you can get involved with The Lopez Family Foundation, dedicated to improving the health and well-being of women and children.

Videos

Selena Movie Trailer
www.youtube.com/watch?v=urAy7RJIWUs
Visit this link to see the movie trailer for *Selena*, Jennifer's breakout role.

Jennifer Lopez on the *Ellen DeGeneres Show*
www.youtube.com/watch?v=Lu6_HDX6_aE
In this 2014 interview, Jennifer talks with Ellen DeGeneres about family, *American Idol*, and more.

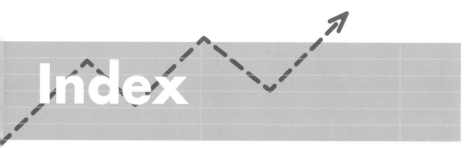

Index

About the Author

Kate Shoup has authored more than twenty-five books and has edited many more. The subjects have included computers and crafts, business, and grammar. Kate has also co-written a feature-length screenplay (and starred in the ensuing film) and worked as the sports editor for NUVO Newsweekly. When not writing, Kate, an IndyCar fanatic, loves to ski, read, and ride her motorcycle. She lives in Indianapolis, Indiana, with her husband, her daughter, and their dog. To learn more about Kate and her work, visit www.kateshoup.com.